Introduction

This book is about experiences of childhood between the years of 1837 and 1901, the 64 years which make up the reign of Queen Victoria. Children then made up a much larger proportion of the population than is the case today. In 1881, nearly half the population of England and Wales was under the age of 20 and a quarter was under the age of 10.

In this book you will find extracts which illustrate various aspects of Victorian childhood. When you read them, try to compare the experiences of Victorian children with yours today. Always remember that many different lifestyles existed and that the experiences of Victorian children differed widely according to the social class of the family to which they belonged, the year in which they were born – because many improvements took place within the 64-year period – the area where they lived and whether they were male or female. Whilst some children suffered from long working hours and others enjoyed the security of a wealthy home, many children, as today, experienced a happy, "normal" life somewhere in between these two extremes.

Family life was considered to be very important. Queen Victoria and her husband, Prince Albert, had nine children and for many people theirs seemed a perfect example of a happy family. Large families meant that children had no need to look further than their own home for amusements. Brothers and sisters were usually available for lessons, games, sports and home-made entertainment. Parents expected the greatest respect from their children, who were to be "seen but not heard" when in their presence. This was especially important when with their father. He was considered to be the ruling head of the household and his word was rarely challenged. Many parents believed in firm discipline and considered corporal punishment for bad behaviour to be essential if a child was to grow into a responsible, moral adult. "Spare the rod and spoil the child" was a saying that many Victorian parents and teachers firmly believed.

For most of the nineteenth century many children had no formal education. The 1870 Forster Education Act made provision for more schools to be built in areas which lacked them. This meant, in theory, that every child should have been able to attend school. In practice, however, many parents were unable to afford the school fees or to manage without the extra money that their working children contributed to the family income. Schooling did not become compulsory until 1880 and free state elementary education was not available until 1891.

Today, many opportunities exist in schools for both sexes, but during the early years of Victoria's reign, those girls receiving an education were treated very differently from boys. Girls were trained exclusively for the role of housewife and mother. An education more ambitious or academic was considered inappropriate to their future. This attitude prevailed until the end of the century, when a group of determined middle-class women made attempts to reform girls' education by introducing more academic subjects.

For most of Victoria's reign child labour was an accepted part of life. Partly because of this there was no sharp distinction between childhood and adulthood. Today, childhood is officially considered to end at 18. During the last century it was often seen to end as soon as regular work began. For some children this was when they were only five or six. Other Victorian children suffered because they were unwanted and neglected paupers, forced to spend their lives on the streets. These destitute children often turned to crime as a means of survival. The majority of people were unaware of the plight of these poor children, but some wealthy individuals realized that they could do something to help. Dr Barnardo was one philanthropist who provided shelter for pauper children. Others such as Lord Shaftesbury tried to improve the working conditions of the young.

Victorian children were very susceptible to illness and disease. Many died from complaints that offer no threat to us today. Most families would have experienced the loss of at least one baby or child. Infant mortality was particularly high in some industrial areas. A report written in 1891 showed that, even then, one-tenth of the children born in factory towns would die before they reached the age of five. But, towards the end of the century, the lifestyle of most children had improved in some way. Better working conditions, shorter working hours, a healthier diet, more public concern for the welfare of children and the provision of free education had all played a part.

There is a wealth of material available on the subject of Victorian childhood. If you are interested you can find out more about the life of children in your area. I hope this book will be the start of a successful study of your nineteenth-century counterparts.

Funeral card of a child who died from scarlet fever in 1881. Note his age. One of his sisters died from the same disease six days later.

≡ Useful Sources ≡

1. PEOPLE

a) *Victorian people* You may be fortunate enough to meet an elderly person who was born in the nineteenth century. He or she may remember being a child and be happy to talk to you about it. It might be useful to prepare some questions to help the conversation along. You could record the interview on a cassette tape recorder and transcribe your recording later. Other people may remember stories and memories that their parents shared with them about growing up in Victorian times and be willing to tell you about them.

b) *Librarians* The librarian in the reference or the local history section of your main public library will be able to suggest similar sources to the ones mentioned in this book but relevant to your area.

c) *Head teachers* If your school building is Victorian or you know of another in your locality which is, then the head teacher may still have the school log books. These will give you a valuable insight into daily school life.

2. VISUAL MATERIAL

a) *Old photographs* Many families keep old photograph albums. Ask your relatives and friends

A studio portrait of a Victorian father and two of his children. Family photographs like this help us to learn about the appearance of nineteenth-century children.

Finding Out About
VICTORIAN CHILDHOOD

Pamela Harper

B.T. Batsford Ltd, London

Contents

Introduction	3
Useful Sources	4
Family Life	6
Rich Children	8
Poor Children	10
Working Children	12
A London Child	14
In the Country	16
School	18
Lessons	20
Boarding Schools	22
Church and Sunday Schools	24
Clothes and Appearance	26
Toys and Games	28
Hobbies	30
Entertainment	32
Children's Literature	34
Celebrations	36
Going on Holiday	38
Diet	40
Illness and Disease	42
Map	44
Difficult Words	45
Date List	46
Places to Visit	46
Biographical Notes	47
Book List	47
Index	48

Cover Illustrations

The colour photograph is of Queen Victoria, Prince Albert and the Royal Family (Michael Rawcliffe); the black and white photograph on the left is "she brings her little 'brudder' for some breakfast" from *The Expansion of a Mission* by Rev. J. Gregory Mantle (Michael Rawcliffe); the advertisement on the right is for a High School for Boys from *Strong's Directory of Bromley, Kent, 1892* (Bromley Public Library).

Typeset by Tek-Art Ltd, Kent
and printed in Great Britain by
R J Acford Ltd
Chichester, Sussex
for the publishers
B.T. Batsford Ltd,
4 Fitzhardinge Street
London W1H 0AH

ISBN 0 7134 4755 9

ACKNOWLEDGMENTS

The Author and Publishers would like to thank the following for permission to reproduce copyright material: Bethnal Green Museum of Childhood for the photographs on pages 9, 29 and 31; Bromley Public Library for the photographs on pages 22 and 32; Caliban Books for extracts on pages 31, 32 and 37 from *A Small Boy in the Sixties* by George Sturt; Cambridge University Press for extracts on pages 16-17, 20 and 35 from *Joseph Ashby of Tysoe 1859-1919* by M.K. Ashby; Chatto and Windus for extracts on pages 6-7 and 41 from *Life As We Have Known It*, ed. M. Llewelyn Davies; Bernard Cheese for the photographs on pages 37 and 39; the Communist Party Library for the photograph on page 5; Faber & Faber for extracts on pages 9, 26 and 30 from *Period Piece* by Gwen Raverat; Farnborough Primary School for the photograph on page 36; the Governors of Caterham School for the extract on pages 22-3 and 38 from *a History of Caterham School*; Mary Harper for the frontispiece and the photographs on pages 4 and 43; J. Jones for the photograph on page 30. Kent Archives Office for extracts on pages 8, 21 and 36 from the diaries of Eva Knatchbull Hugessen; Liverpool City Library for the photograph on page 12; John Murray from the extract on pages 26-7 from *Life Among the Troubridges* by J. Hope Nicholson; Oxford University Press for extracts on pages 12, 28 and 30 from *Lark Rise to Candleford* by Flora Thompson, on *continued on p. 48.*

they can help you. Museums, record offices and libraries may have photographic collections.

a) *Objects* Some museums have sections on Victorian games, toys and books which you would find useful. Other museums have reconstructions of schoolrooms and nurseries. Samples of children's school work may also be on display. For more details see the Places to Visit section at the end of this book.

b) *Illustrations* Many examples are to be found in contemporary newspapers and magazines as well as in Victorian books (many published for children). Always remember that an illustration represents an artist's interpretation of events and, therefore, may be biased and not entirely accurate.

This includes a list of the local schools in each area. Kelly's Post Office Directory is one of the most comprehensive.

c) *Advertisements* Much can be found out about schools, fashions, holidays and shops in advertisements found in newspapers, magazines and directories.

d) *Diaries and autobiographies* You may find one written by a local person. Look either in the local history section of your main public library or in the local record office. If you wish to visit this office it is best to write first to the County Archivist explaining what material you hope to see and find out about.

e) *Documents* Useful documents to read include Sunday School records, school log books and

An attic occupied by a family of ten in Bethnal Green, London. Marx described London as "the first place in overcrowded habitations, absolutely unfit for human beings".

3. WRITTEN SOURCES

a) *Newspapers and periodicals* Your main public library may have nineteenth-century editions of your town's local newspapers. These are useful for accounts of school board meetings, Sunday school events and descriptions of special occasions such as the Diamond Jubilee celebrations of 1897.

b) *Victorian directories* Local directories give detailed information about each town and village.

workhouse records. These may be found in libraries and record offices, or they may still be in the possession of local schools and churches.

f) *Census material* The first national census was in 1801, but the later ones contain more information. From 1851 the census returns list interesting facts about each member of the family who was in residence on census day. It is possible to find out the age, occupation and place of birth of each listed person. Because of these personal contents, census material is only made available 100 years after it is taken. The original returns are kept at the Public Record Office in London, but your main library may have the returns for your area on microfilm.

Family Life

Victorian families were much larger than those of today. A large family living comfortably in a large house was seen to be a symbol of security and prosperity. Wealthy parents were able to afford a nanny or nursemaid to assist in the upbringing of their children. These children may only have seen their parents once a day and often grew very fond of the servants who cared for them. Older children in poor families frequently had to care for the younger members while their parents were out working. For these children life would be a constant struggle.

FATHERS

Catherine Edwards was born in 1888 into a rich family living in Worthing. Here she recalls her relationship with her father:

> I was allowed to walk with my father. He liked a two hour walk in the evenings. I used to have to be booted – we had boots in those days not shoes – and be very tidy and neat. I had to be waiting and ready for him to call out when he was ready for this walk. We used to walk about two or three miles along the Lancing road towards Brighton and perhaps not speak a word to each other, but he said I was pleasant to walk with because I didn't talk and I didn't get my boots dirty. We only had meals with him on certain days of the week. He would eat with us usually on Sundays, but the rest of the week he would have his meals in his own room and we were not allowed to disturb him.

This is typical of the Victorian age. Fathers tended not to spend much time with their children and expected to be treated with the greatest respect. Virtually all important decisions relating to the family were made by the father. It was not until the changing attitudes towards the role of women in the twentieth century that mothers have been able to influence important family matters.

An illustration from a children's periodical 1872, romanticizing the fact that many poor children had to care for and feed their younger brothers and sisters.

FAMILY SIZE

In *Life As We Have Known It*, published in 1931, a member of the Women's Co-operative Guild recorded her memories of childhood:

DAILY ROUTINE

The following advice to middle-class parents comes from the very successful *Mrs. Beeton's Every Day Cookery and Housekeeping Book* (1865);

> **Children's nursery hours should be as follows:– All out of bed at seven, all dressed and sitting down to breakfast at eight, nine o'clock should see the little troop out of doors in garden, in park, or on country roads. Two hours' walk in the morning and two in the afternoon is necessary in fine weather. After the 20th of October all children under six should be indoors after three o'clock: this rule should be continued until spring days again come around.**

Why do you think children under six had to be indoors by three o'clock? How has this routine changed for children of pre-school age today?

> **I was born in Bethnal Green, April 9th 1855. . . . I was my mother's seventh child, and seven more were born after me – fourteen in all – which made my mother a perfect slave. Generally speaking, she was either expecting a baby to be born or had one at the breast. At the time there was eight of us the oldest was not big enough to get ready to go to school without help.**

How many children are there in the largest family that you know of? Imagine living in your present home with possibly eight or nine other brothers and sisters. What sort of changes would have to be made to your present lifestyle?

THE FAMILY AS A WORKING UNIT

In his survey titled *London Labour and the London Poor* (1861) Henry Mayhew drew attention to the plight of families in which all the members young and old had to work together in order to survive. Here is the statement of one worker:

> **The most of us has got large families. We put the children to work as soon as we can. My little girl began about six, but about eight or nine is the usual age. . . . The most of the cabinet-makers [makers of furniture] of the East end have from five to six in family, and they are generally all at work for them. . . . You see, we couldn't live if it wasn't for the labour of our children, though it makes 'em – poor little things! – old people long before they are growed up.**

In what ways do you think the children were able to assist their families?

FOSTER PARENTS

For children without a family the workhouse often became home, but the practice of placing homeless children with foster parents was widespread enough in 1877 for the Guardians of the Bromley Union to receive a letter from the Local Government Board:

> **. . . calling attention of the Guardians to the practice of placing Orphans and Deserted Children in homes in the Union or Parish to which they belong and paying the foster parents a weekly allowance for their maintenance. . .**

In what ways would the foster parents have benefited from this arrangement?

Rich Children

Rich children usually lived in their own nursery quarter, separate from the rest of the house. They were cared for initially by a nanny and nursemaid. Tutors and governesses were employed to educate the children. Not all children enjoyed the same privileges as their parents. Some families considered it right for their children to suffer some hardship while they were young. Life in the nursery could be very austere with hardly any heating, a very plain and boring diet and strict discipline.

FAMILY PURSUITS

The following extracts from the diary of Ellen Buxton were written in the 1860s. Contrast the description of her activities with those of the poor described in the next chapter.

> **Dec. 23. 1861.** This afternoon we went to the Alms houses near here and gave to each of the people half a pound of tea and a pound of sugar, which they liked very much.

> **Mar. 29. 1862.** This afternoon we all went to dig up primroses at Warlies. . . . As we went we ate some biscuits and milk, because we were very hungry. All Sunday the two hampers were standing outside the hall door and they looked very beautiful, quite full of primroses.
>
> **Apr. 2nd. 1862.** Today Baby was put into short clothes; she looks so pretty. I think much prettier than when she was in long clothes. She has got the most beautiful little flannel petty coat I ever saw.

Who do you think "we" would have meant?

A THIRTEENTH BIRTHDAY

Eva Knatchbull Hugessen wrote in her diary how she celebrated her thirteenth birthday:

> Saturday 19th December 1874. My thirteenth birthday! ! ! ! ! ! ! I had my presents after prayers. From Mama, a small musical box, which plays four tunes . . . from papa, an awefully jolly horse and carriage for my dolls. Ned, a small water colour paintbox, Kate, Macaulay's lays of ancient rome [a book of poems]. Miss Hugill, a purse, Cecil two boxes of soldiers . . . and some

◀ A carte de visite c. *1890 of a rich boy wearing a velvet suit made fashionable by the publication of* Little Lord Fauntleroy. *This type of portrait was very popular with upper- and middle-class families during the latter half of the century. Many would be printed and given freely to relatives and friends. Compare the clothes worn by this boy with those worn by the children in the next chapter.*

The drawing room of a dolls' house about 1835-8. ➤
Dolls' houses were often miniature versions of real
houses, containing accurately made furniture and
decorations. A rich child's home would probably
contain a room very similar to this one. The aim of a
dolls' house was to teach girls how to run a household
properly.

NANNIES

Like most rich children, Gwen Raverat was cared for
by a nanny when she was young:

> I can never remember being bathed by
> my mother, or even having my hair
> brushed by her, and I should not at all
> have liked it if she had done anything of
> the kind. We did not feel it was her
> place to do such things; though my
> father used to cut our finger-nails with
> his sharp white-handled knife, and that
> felt quite pleasant and proper. Anyhow,
> there was no need for my mother to do
> such things, for Nana hardly ever
> went out, and if she did the housemaid

or the nurserymaid was left in charge of
us. (*Period Piece*, published in 1960)

Nana was the affectionate term the family children
used for their nanny.

NURSERIES

In an article in *Decoration and Furniture of Town
Houses* (1881), it was claimed that nurseries were
often very drab and that an effort should be made to
cheer them up. The following suggestions were
given:

> In the windows of the day nursery there
> should be boxes of flowers . . . to teach
> the little ones of the country, and of the
> nursery rhymes and fairy tales they
> love so well. Let the walls be papered
> with some pleasant paper, in which the
> colours shall be bright and cheerful. . . .
> A band of colour might be made by
> buying some of the Christmas books,
> which Mr. H.S. Marks, R.A., Miss Kate
> Greenaway, and Mr. Walter Crane have
> so charmingly and artistically
> illustrated, and by pasting the scenes in
> regular order and procession, as a kind
> of frieze under the upper band of
> distemper [paint], varnished over to
> protect from dirt.

> sweets. Charlie gave me a little ivory
> case, with a sort of paper snake in it.
> Aunt Cecelia sent me a book called the
> Pioneers. Jemima sent me a muff and
> comforter for my dolls. . . . In the
> morning Cecil and I went out and
> snowballed a little. In the afternoon we
> played in the New Drawing Room, the
> Billiard table has come and is being
> unpacked in the Billiard room. We all
> dined together at seven. My cake was
> pretty to look at, but was not very nice.

What games and amusements were popular in the
Hugessen family?

See if you can find examples of Kate Greenaway's
illustrations.

Poor Children

Life for the poor was a constant struggle to make ends meet. Parents could not afford to send their families to school and so the children were usually unable to read or write. As soon as the children were old enough, they were sent out to work. Others begged for money or food. Some turned to crime. There were also many destitute children on the streets with no-one to turn to. After the Poor Law Amendment Act of 1834, destitute families wanting relief were forced into the workhouse. Many people struggled to survive outside as they knew that once inside their families would be split up. Inside they would also be forced to wear workhouse clothes and have their hair cropped short. Some children were fortunate to be cared for in charitable homes set up by religious organizations or by individuals such as Dr Barnardo. He opened his first home in 1867 with the motto "no child ever turned away" written over the door.

PICKPOCKETS

A young pickpocket in London told Henry Mayhew why he thought so many boys had become vagrant pickpockets:

Why sir, if boys runs away, and has to shelter in low lodging houses – and many runs away from cruel treatment at home – they meet there with boys such as me, or as bad, and the devil soon lays his hands on them. . . . I think the fathers of such boys either ill-treat them, or neglect them; and so they run away.

This boy then went on to say what he thought would become of him:

Transportation. If a boy has great luck he may carry on for eight years. Three or four years is the common run, but transportation is what he's sure to come to in the end. (*London Labour and the London Poor*, 1861)

To where would he have been transported?

A group of children playing in the slums of London. Note their clothing and footwear and the rubbish in the road where they are playing.

TRAINING AND EDUCATION OF PAUPER CHILDREN

In his social survey of London, *Seven Curses of London* (1869), James Greenwood quotes a Mr Bentley who said that pauper children:

. . . must either steal or starve in the streets, or the State must take charge of them. It may further be affirmed that, in a strictly commercial point of view, it is more economical to devote a certain amount in education and systematic training than by allowing them to grow up in the example of their parents and

Paupers who applied to the parish for aid had to get themselves to the workhouse no matter how far away it might be. Lucy Luck describes how her family entered the workhouse:

> ... now the workhouse belonging to Tring was five miles away, and some sort of conveyance was provided for my crippled sister, but my mother had to get there as best she could with the rest of us others. She started to walk there. ... I remember there was a man with a heavy cart going down the road, and he took us part of the way, until he turned up another road and then we walked on until we got to a school not far from the Union. There my mother sat down on the steps with one of us on each side of her, and one in her arms, crying bitterly over us before she took us into the Union. (quoted in *Useful Toil* by J. Burnett, published in 1974)

Can you think of reasons why Lucy's mother would have been crying?

WORKHOUSE RULES

Inmates were expected to abide by the rules of the workhouse and any variance was punished, as the following extract shows. It is taken from the minutes of the Meeting of the Board of Guardians of the Bromley Union 1861.

> Martha Wisby aged sixteen, and Sarah Smith aged fifteen, persisted in wearing their hair contrary to the regulations of the House after repeated admonitions [warnings] from the master that their conduct would be reported to the Board. The Board by a special direction, ordered that Martha Wisby be confined in a separate room for twenty-four hours, and Sarah Smith for twelve hours and kept on bread and water.

EDUCATION

Some workhouse children were educated inside the Union whilst others were sent to local schools. Children in the Bromley Union workhouse were frequently admitted to Farnborough Mixed School which was close by. This is one of many similar entries made in the school log book:

> I admitted a girl, Emily Jackman, aged nine years from the workhouse. She cannot read or write the letters of the alphabet.

The Head complained of the poor standard of work produced by these children. Why do you think their education had suffered?

workhouse companions, to render their permanent support, either in a prison or a workhouse, a burden on the industrious classes.

Care was always taken, though, not to make conditions too comfortable for the poor:

> In no case should their comfort be better than, nor in fact as good as, an industrious labourer has within his reach.

Why was this precaution thought to be necessary? Why did Bentley think it a good investment to spend money on some kind of education for pauper children?

Working Children

In the 1840s, as a result of the findings of the Children's Employment Commission, steps were taken to improve the working conditions of children. The main aims were to reduce the hours that children could legally work and to prevent very young children from being employed at all. Many parents complained, though, that their families would starve if they were deprived of the children's income. Some employers ignored the new law altogether and made it easy for children to lie about their age and, therefore, to continue work.

GOING INTO SERVICE

Flora Thompson was brought up in a small village in the 1870s. In *Lark Rise to Candleford*, published in 1939, she describes how many of her friends entered domestic service at an early age:

> **After the girls left school at ten or eleven, they were usually kept at home for a year to help with the younger children, then places were found for them locally in the households of tradesmen, schoolmasters, stud grooms or farm bailiffs. . . . The first places were called 'petty places' and looked upon as stepping-stones to better things. . . . The wages were small, often only a shilling a week; but the remuneration [reward] did not end with the money payment . . . the Christmas gift of a best frock or a winter coat was common.**

After entering service some girls may have only seen their families again during their annual fortnight's holiday. How would you feel about leaving your family and friends at such an early age? Would parents have encouraged their daughters more than their sons to leave home to find employment?

AT WORK IN MANCHESTER

The following extract shows the extent to which children still worked longer hours than those set for factory workers by the Ten Hours Act of 1847. The boys mentioned all lived in the Manchester area.

> **. . . is ten years of age. Works at a foundry for thirteen hours a day and earns 2s 6d a week, which his parents take.**
> **. . . is fourteen years of age. Can read well. Works at a brick croft from dark to dark for which he has 5s a week.**
> **. . . is thirteen years of age, and works in a machine-shop from six in the morning till eight and nine, and sometimes ten o'clock at night. Has 4s a week. Would rather work fewer hours; but his father sends him, and takes the money.** (Angus Bethune Reach, *Manchester and the Textile Districts in 1849*)

Many children worked in the streets selling matches and newspapers or helping in markets. This photograph, taken by Thomas Burke c. 1895, shows a group of shoeblacks (shoe cleaners) who worked in the streets of Liverpool.

BRICK- AND TILE-MAKING INDUSTRIES

As a child of seven in the 1840s George Smith had worked in the brickmaking industry. In *The Cry of the Children from the Brick-Yards of England*, (1879) he wrote that the working conditions had still not changed:

> The children were of various ages, from nine to twelve, but mostly nine to ten. They were of both sexes, and in a half naked state. Their employment consisted in carrying the damp clay on their heads to the brickmakers, and carrying the made bricks to the 'floors' on which they are placed to dry. Their employment lasts thirteen hours daily during which they traverse a distance of about twenty miles.

The Brick-yard Act of 1871 went some way to improve these conditions, but it was a difficult act to enforce. Why do you think this was so?

Where might the 14-year-old have learnt to read so well? Find out which industries in your area employed children during the last century.

HALF-TIMERS

When the following Report was printed in the *Bromley Record* in 1877, legislation had made it possible for children over the age of 11 to be granted half-time certificates.

> Many of the applications [for half-time certificates] . . . concerned scholars under twelve years of age, and the Board refused to allow children of such an age exemption from full attendance. It was pointed out that the age limit was fixed at eleven years, but the chairman explained that the Board had to determine whether a child was to be 'beneficially and necessarily' employed, before they allowed any scholar to become a half-timer. It was also suggested that the standard required to be passed before children were eligible to obtain the certificate might be raised.

Do you think half-time at school and half-time at work is a good idea or not?

USEFUL EMPLOYMENT IN THE WORKHOUSE

A report of 1878 stated that when the Bromley workhouse children were not at school, they were expected to be:

> . . . placed under the care and training of one of the following officers.
> . . . a Male Cook and Baker . . . who cooks all food and makes bread.
> . . . a Male Labor Master . . . who makes and repairs boots, shoes and slippers.
> . . . a Female Industrial Trainer . . . who makes whole of clothes for establishment so girls not only receive instruction in ordinary work of a General Domestic Servant, but are taught needlework thoroughly.

Apart from considering the future employment of the children in the workhouse, what other, more immediate, effect might this extra workforce have had on the running of the institution?

A London Child

The social problems of the capital were brought to the attention of the public by a series of books and reports written by men such as Henry Mayhew, James Greenwood and Charles Booth. They were particularly concerned with the plight of the poor. Many investigative journalists travelled into the slum areas of London to find out from first-hand experience how bad life really was. Many people lived in overcrowded "rookeries", which were groups of large old houses built around courtyards and surrounded by mazes of alleys.

PAUPER POPULATION

In *The Seven Curses of London* (1869) James Greenwood writes:

> ...it is an accepted fact that, daily, winter and summer, within the limits of our vast and wealthy city of London, there wander, destitute of proper guardianship, food, clothing, or employment, a hundred thousand boys and girls in fair trading for the treadmill and the oakum shed, and finally for Portland and the convict's mark.

What do you think Portland and the convict's mark referred to? The next extract details Greenwood's answer to the problem.

> We cannot deal with our babies of the gutter effectually and with any reasonable chance of success, until we have separated them entirely from their home. We may tame and teach them to feed out of our hand, and to repeat after us the alphabet, and even words of two and three syllables...but they can never be other than restless

LOOKING FOR A BETTER LIFE

Many people came to live in London believing that the "streets were paved with gold". Amongst these were many young orphans. One boy told Henry Mayhew his reasons for coming to London:

> I came to London to beg, thinking I could get more there than anywhere else, hearing that London was such a good place. I begged; but sometimes wouldn't get a farthing in a day; often walking about the streets all night. . . . I never slept in a bed since I've been in London: I am sure I haven't: I generally slept under the dry arches in West

Window shopping outside a London coffee bar c. 1900. Do these boys look as if they can afford the advertised prices?

and ungovernable and unclean birds, while they inhabit the vile old parent nest.

Unfortunately, Greenwood fails to recommend alternative homes to the slums that he wishes to see abolished.

Street, where they're building houses – I mean the arches for the cellars.
(*London Labour and the London Poor*, 1861)

What were the alternatives to begging if an orphan child was to survive?

MUDLARKS

A "mudlark" was someone who retrieved articles from the mud of the River Thames at low tide. Henry Mayhew wrote an account of their activities. Here is is description of one boy:

He had taken to mud-larking he said, because his clothes were too bad for him to look for anything better. He worked everyday with twenty or thirty other boys, who might all be seen at daybreaks with their trousers tucked up, groping about, and picking up the pieces of coal from the mud on the banks of the Thames. He went into the river up to his knees, and in searching the mud he often ran pieces of glass and long nails into his feet. When this was the case, he went home and dressed the wounds, but returned to the river-side directly. (*London Labour and the London Poor*, 1861)

The coal he collected would have fallen from the Thames coal-barges. It was sold to the poor of the area at one penny per pot. A pot held 14 pounds.

CITY CELEBRATIONS

Rich and poor children alike would have been able to experience many free shows or parades. Here is

PEA SOUPERS

Londoners suffered many thick fogs every winter. In his autobiography, Edward Thomas recalls many such "pea soupers" during his childhood in the 1890s. Unaware of their dangers at the time, he describes them as exciting times.

People went about with lanterns and you could get lost, or if not you could pretend to, and stay out late. It was good also to belong to a search party and, perhaps, in spite of a lantern, turn out to be lost yourself or back at your starting place. Clapham Common on those foggy nights was in many ways like desert undiscovered country, yet perfectly harmless. (*The Childhood of Edward Thomas*, published in 1938)

Why did the city suffer from so many thick fogs and why would they have been dangerous? Try to find out when the last dangerous fog in London was.

Molly Hughes' description of the festivities in the city in November, taken from *A London Child of the 1870s*:

November meant fogs . . . and perhaps 'doing without a fire' because it was not quite cold enough. The one excitement to be certain of was the Lord Mayor's Show, coinciding with the Prince of Wales's birthday, and a school holiday. The boys always went . . . they always brought home for me a little book, that opened out to nearly a yard of coloured pictures displaying all the features of the Show. This was called 'A Penny Panorama of the Lord Mayor's Show' and the name pleased me so much that for days afterwards I would go about the house pretending to be a hawker. . .

In the Country

Apart from the advantages of fresh air and open surroundings, life in the country could be just as grim as in the overcrowded city slums. Many children were employed to work in agricultural gangs moving from farm to farm. They were hired and led by adult gang leaders who arranged the work with the farmers.

WORKING ON THE LAND

Many reports on the employment of children in agriculture were written for Parliament during the 1860s. The following extract is taken from the *Second Report of the Royal Commission on the Employment of Children, Young Persons and Women in Agriculture* (1868-69):

> **The ordinary farm operations in which the youngest children are employed are bird-minding, minding cows, sheep,**

The temporary home of a hop-picking family. Notice the lack of facilities for washing, bathing and cooking. Try to imagine the living conditions inside the building.

> **and pigs, picking and gathering potatoes, and collecting acorns. . . . The special occupations in which they are engaged are hop-picking . . . and . . . apple picking. . . . As a general rule there is work to be done by children . . . throughout the whole summer, and education in this neighbourhood suffers in consequence.**

The following extract is taken from the Log Book of Farnborough Mixed School in Kent. It was written on 28 September 1896.

> **The Tug Mutton children returned to**

GLEANING

Whole families worked on the land during haymaking and the corn harvest. When the harvesting was over, families were allowed on to the land to glean for themselves.

school from hop-picking after an absence from June 6th last and too backward for their previous standard [class].

Do you think the parents of these children would have been concerned about their progress in school? At what other times of the year do you think these children might have been absent?

SUMMER EVENTS

The school summer term extended into August so that the holiday would coincide with the village harvest. Before the schools closed an annual treat was usually enjoyed by the pupils, as in this log book from a village school in West Bergholt, Essex:

... women and children waited at the gate to exercise, in the form of a privilege, one of the last of the old customary rights of the pre-enclosure days. Each woman, with the children she had been able to bring, took a 'land' or ploughing ridge, laid out a sheet with a stone at each corner, and then the whole company began to move slowly up the ridges, all the figures bending, hands deep in the stubble, 'leasing' fallen ears. Each gleaner had a linsey-woolsey bag hanging from her waist. Tiny boys and girls had tiny bags...
(*Joseph Ashby of Tysoe, 1859-1919*)

The corn that had been gleaned would be sent to the miller to be ground. From this flour several weeks' bread could be made.

August 5th 1897 ... As the rector has left the parish and no successor at present in residence it was feared that the annual School Treat would this year have to be abandoned. However through the exertion of the master and Mrs. Wythe enough money was raised not only to provide the scholars with an ample repast, but also to entertain the parents and engage the West Bergholt Brass Band...

Why do you think the School Treat was normally dependent on the local rector?

LIVING CONDITIONS

An Assistant Commissioner collecting evidence for the 1867-78 *Royal Commission on Women and Children in Agriculture* met a shepherd's wife in Dorset. She describes to him the living conditions of her family:

... There are seven [children] living at home with me now. Our third bedroom was put up the summer before last. Before that time, we had only two, and we used all of us to sleep in them, at one time there were thirteen or fourteen of us. ... We live on potatoes, bread and pig-meat; we often sit down to dry bread. ... We never have a bit of milk. They are very fond of butter. We drink tea...

These crowded living conditions and this simple diet were common for most agricultural families.

School

A great variety of schools existed throughout the nineteenth century. Middle- and upper-class parents were able to send their children to fee-paying Grammar, Public and Private schools. Poor children had schools provided either by the Church of England (National schools), or by the nonconformist churches (British and Foreign schools). Dame schools, Workhouse schools, Charity schools and Ragged schools also existed for poor children. Older pupils, called monitors, often assisted teachers in these schools. After the 1870 Forster Education Act provision was made for new schools to be built in areas where there were not enough voluntary schools. Local areas were to appoint School Boards to be responsible for building these schools which became known as Board schools. Victorian directories will tell you how many different types of schools existed in your area.

In 1880 education was made compulsory but, as we saw in the previous chapters, there was often a high rate of absenteeism as many parents preferred to put their children out to work rather than send them to school.

RULES AND DISCIPLINE

The Headmaster of Boughton Monchelsea School in Kent recorded this entry in the school log book in 1872:

October 29. No talking allowed in the future in school.
October 30. School very quiet today, only two cases of talking. Emily Cole and Ernest Thompsett confined to the school for one month.
November 5. I find the school work much better under strict

INSPECTORS' REPORT

In 1862 the Revised Code of Education introduced a "payment by results" scheme. Education grants were to be granted to schools if attendance and the standard of the pupils' work met the requirements of inspectors. Visiting inspectors conducted one-day examinations in schools and copies of their reports were written in the school log book. The following report is from a small village school in Essex. It was written in 1892.

Mixed School. The general results of the examination are only pretty fair. Reading requires more teaching, also Spelling and Composition, and there is a great want of intelligence in

discipline. I have had no occasion to speak today about talking.
November 6.
Ernest Thompsett punished for talking.

Try to imagine life in your school without any talking. Would you learn more if you always worked in silence? What do you think was meant by the punishment "confined to the school"? A further insight into school rules is given in another entry into the same log book.

January 29. Orders were given last week that no child would be admitted after the Bell had rung – and the door would be locked punctually at nine and two o'clock. Bertha Lettham, George Trowel and Edmund Folly punished for going home on finding the door locked at five past nine.

Why was it necessary to lock the doors? Why would some country children be late for school?

Arithmetic, both written and oral. Miss Rose Oakley must improve in her teaching if she is to be again recognised under Article 68. The urinal accommodation [lavatories] for the boys is very insufficient.

Try to imagine the teacher's worry as each child was tested on his or her work. Remember that the school grant and the teacher's salary were dependent on good results.

RAGGED SCHOOLS

The Ragged School Union was formed in 1844. Its aim was to set up new, free schools for children who were too "ragged" or poor to attend other schools. Ragged schools flourished in urban slum areas. Children attended them in the evening after working all day. A young boy told Henry Mayhew about his experiences in a Ragged school:

... I went to have a warm and see what it was like. When I got there the master was very kind to me. They used to give us tea-parties, and to keep us quiet they used to show us the magic lanterns. I soon got to like going there and went

GOING TO SCHOOL IN WASHINGTON VILLAGE

Thomas Jordan describes his early memories of school life in the 1890s in Tyne and Wear:

I commenced school when I was three years old. I was in a dress the same as the girls, a petticoat. Every morning, my older sister and I had to walk a mile and a half to school in Washington village.... There were no particular

SCHOOL FEES

Schooling did not become free until the 1891 Act. The *Beckenham Journal* of November 1876 reported the local School Board's approved new scale of fees:

3d. per week per child, except when more than two in a family attend, when a reduction of 1d per week would be made after the first child, thus – one child 3d. per week, two ditto 6d., three ditto 7d., four ditto 9d., and so on. Five hours in each day would actually be devoted to instruction with an interval of a few minutes for recreation.

How much would a family with six children of school age have to pay each week?

every night for six months. There was about forty or fifty boys in the school. The most of them was thieves...
(*London Labour and the London Poor*, 1861)

What did this pupil like about his Ragged school? Do you think he learnt much there?

places to have a mid-day meal. In the summertime we sat on the village green and had the food given to us by mother. We would get a can of cold milk for twopence at the farm nearby to wash down our food. In the winter the school mistress allowed us to warm our can of tea on the school fire and we could sit at our school bench and have it there.
(Quoted in *Useful Toil* by J. Burnett, published in 1974)

Try to find out when the schools' meals service began.

Lessons

Joseph Ashby started at his village school in 1864 at the age of five.

> **Right up the school, through all the six standards [classes] you did almost nothing except reading, writing and arithmetic. What a noise there used to be! Several children would be reading aloud, teachers scolding, infants reciting, all waxing [growing] louder and louder until the master rang the bell on his desk and the noise slid down to a lower note and less volume.** (*Joseph Ashby of Tysoe 1859-1919*)

What does this extract tell you about the curriculum of this school, the teaching methods employed by the teachers and the organization of the classes?

OBJECT LESSONS

The Log Book of Farnborough Infants School in Kent contains a proposed list of Object Lessons for the year ending 31 January 1898. An object was chosen for discussion in class. The infants were expected to remember any facts learnt in this discussion and were tested on them at a later date.

Class II

Nat. Hist.	Objects	Phen. of Nature
1. Bear.	1. an Egg.	1. The Sky.
2. Elephant.	2. an Apple.	2. The Rainbow.
3. Reindeer.	3. a Tree.	3. Winter.
4. Lion.	4. Teaplant.	4. Ice.
5. Goat.	5. Water.	
6. Squirrel.	6. Coal.	**Trades**
7. Swallow.		1. Postman.
8. Eagle.		2. Baker.

Lessons in school were usually conducted in large groups and in a very formal manner. The curriculum was often rather limited as the "payment by results" system meant that many schools would only teach those subjects that would earn them a grant. Lessons were not meant to be enjoyed by the pupils. The entire class was expected to progress at the same rate regardless of the children's different interests and abilities.

RECITATIONS

Pupils were often expected to learn extracts from literature by heart.

> **During my first term I hardly ever had a good night's sleep. Every morning before Prayers we had to recite to the form mistress or one of the monitors a piece of poetry – a different kind for each day of the week: on Monday it was verses of a Psalm; on Tuesdays, English; on Wednesday, French; On Thursday, German; on Friday, Latin.**

You can read more about Molly Hughes' schooldays at the North London Collegiate School in *A London Girl of the 1880s.*

Why do you think this method of learning was favoured by the teachers? Ask any elderly relatives or friends you know if they can remember learning in this way.

Photographs, paintings or models of the objects were shown to the children as a form of visual aid. How appropriate do you think the objects were for infants? These lessons proved to be very popular. Can you think why? Would this still be the case if they were used today?

CHAP. VII.

SWITZERLAND.

1. SWIT'-ZER-LAND is a small, but romantic country, adjoining the alps, the highest mountains in Eu'rope. Its population is about two millions two hundred thousand.

2. The principal towns of Swit'-zer-land are Berne, the capital, * Neuf-cha-tel', +Zu'-rich, and Ge-ne'-va.

3. Swit'-zer-land is distinguished for its beautiful and picturesque scenery, consisting of lofty mountains and dreadful precipices, intermixed with delightful valleys, rivers, and lakes. It is divided into twenty-two districts, or can'-tons.

4. The principal lakes of Swit'-zer-land are Con'-stance, Lu-cerne', *Neuf-cha-tel, and Ge-ne'-va.

5. The Swiss are a robust people, noted for the simplicity of their manners, and their love of liberty.

HOLLAND.

6. HOL'LAND is a small commercial Kingdom, lying to the east of Eng'-land, from which it is separated by the North Sea. It is divided into seven provinces.

---

* Noo-shat-tel.   + Zu-rik.

and contains about two millions and a half of inhabitants.

7. Holland is a very flat country, lying in some places below the level of the sea, which is kept from overflowing the land by dikes or banks of earth. The soil is highly cultivated, and very productive both in corn and pasture.

8. Am'-ster-dam, the capital, is chiefly built upon wooden piles, and contains many magnificent buildings. It has broad canals running through the streets, with rows of trees on each side, and a good coach-road. It contains 200,000 inhabitants.

9. The other principal towns of Hol'-land, are Hague, Rot'-ter-dam and Ley'-den. Hague, the principal residence of the nobility, is distinguished for the elegance of its buildings, Rot'-ter-dam for its commerce, and Ley'-den for its university.

10. The chief rivers of Holland are the Rhine and the *Maese.

11. The Dutch are considered slow and heavy, but remarkable for their cleanliness, frugality, and industry. Their religion is the Protestant, under the Presbyterian form. The population of Holland is about three millons.

BELGIUM.

12. BEL'-GI-UM, a small Kingdom to

* Maiz.

GOVERNESSES AND HOME TUTORS

Wealthy children were either sent away to private schools or were educated at home by a tutor or governess. Eva Knatchbull Hugessen came from a wealthy family who lived in Kent. Here is the entry from her diary for May 1873, written while she was staying in London.

The lessons we have been having are these . . . German, with Miss Elfrich on mondays and thursdays from half past nine to half past ten. Music, Mr. Couldry, on Saturdays, nine to ten, then we go to the singing class which we went to two years ago, at Lady Salisbury's. Mme. Loyapold is the mistress, on tuesdays and fridays from four to half past five. . . . Miss Hull, the

drawing mistress comes on fridays from half past two to half past three. Then we have . . . a man who makes us do horrid exercises with legs and arms every other day, but it is too hot for that now so we don't go.

Geography for Children *by John Guy, 1853. Note comment 11 about the Dutch! The introduction of this book suggests that children should learn several pages of facts from the book and then answer a list of questions to test their knowledge. Any interpretation of the "facts" would have been considered inappropriate.*

How many different people taught Eva? For how many hours a week did she have lessons? Compare the subjects on your timetable with those that Eva studied. Which timetable do you prefer – yours or Eva's?

Boarding Schools

It became increasingly fashionable to send children to boarding school during the second half of the century when the railways made it possible for children to travel further away from home. The number of boarding schools for boys greatly outnumbered those for girls. The expensive older public schools taught mostly Latin and Greek. Middle-class pressure, however, caused the establishment of new boarding schools with a different curriculum. The emphasis in these schools was on activities that would ensure entrance to the professions. Life was often extremely hard at boarding school. Younger pupils were expected to act like servants to the older boys who often inflicted corporal punishment on their "servants" if they did not obey them.

BOARDERS AND DAY BOYS

In 1888, when he was ten, Edward Thomas went to a private school where;

... there were fifty or sixty boys of from ten to seventeen years of age, perhaps half of them boarders. They were the sons of tradesmen, professional men, moderately well-to-do clerks, and men of small independent means. ... The schoolroom was a large single hall adjacent to the large old brick house where the boarders lived with the headmaster. The three classes under the head and two assistants all occupied the same room, but faced different ways. In the fourth quarter of the room stood the boarders' more substantial desks, where they kept silkworms and white mice. (*The Childhood of Edward Thomas*)

Work out how many boys each master would have been responsible for. How does this compare with the size of the classes in Board schools?

AT BOARDING SCHOOL IN LEWISHAM

In *A History of Caterham School* (1945), one ex-pup remembers boarding school days in Lewisham i the 1850s. The school was founded for the sons c Congregational ministers. It later moved t Caterham, Surrey.

The school life was one of Spartan simplicity. We washed under a pump in

This advertisement for the Middle Class School was placed in the local directory in 1878. Note the diet. Is there any information about the school missing from this advertisement?

xvi.   ADVERTISEMENTS.

MIDDLE CLASS SCHOOL,
BROMLEY COMMON, KEN

Principal:

MR. WM. GAYFER, M.A., F.R.G
Member of the Society of Arts.

Head Master—Mr. JOHN THOMAS CLARK
Resident Foreign Master—Mons. H. O. DONAT
And other Resident Assistants.

Mr. GAYFER prepares Boys thoroughly for Professional or Merc pursuits, also for Examinations by the College of Preceptors and Learned Societies.

EDUCATIONAL COURSE.

Consists of English, Classics, Mathematics, French, German, N Drawing, Book-keeping, Divinity and Drilling.

DOMESTIC ARRANGEMENTS.

Mrs. Wm. and Mrs. GAYFER, Ser., take the immediate charge above, each Pupil's comfort being their special care.

DIET.

Plain, substantial and without limit.

DIVISION OF THE YEAR.

The School year is divided into three equal terms.

TERMS.

These include Board, Laundress, use of Books, Stationery and instru in *all* subjects named, except Music and Drilling, which are extras.

FULL ROARDERS.		Per Term.
9 under 12	... ...	£9 0 0
12 „ 16	... ...	£10 10 0
WEEKLY BOARDERS.		
9 under 12	... ...	£7 7 0
12 „ 16	... ...	£8 8 0
DAY BOARDERS.		
9 under 12	... ...	£5 5 0
12 „ 16	... ...	£6 6 0
DAY PUPILS.		

Each Term £1 1s, and 3s, 6d, per Term for use of Books is charged to Day Bc and Day Pupils.

EXTRAS.

Music, 30s, per Term ; Drilling, Cricket and Football, 10s, per Term the tw

Further information and for Prospectuses, Testimonials, &c., apply to the Pri

a shed on the other side of the playground. It was not relished [enjoyed] in winter. Breakfast and tea consisted of two slices of bread and butter and half a pint of milk and water. Nevertheless we throve on it, and in two years there was not one case of illness. The school library consisted of back numbers of *The Evangelical Magazine* and *Uncle Tom's Cabin.* Newspapers were absolutely barred, and we heard of the Crimean victories when we went home for the holidays.

Why do you think newspapers were barred? See if you can find out what the Crimean victories were.

A GOOD SCHOOL

n 1852 edition of the Victorian magazine ousehold Words contained a description of Bruce astle School in Tottenham:

Everything in the school-room was neat and orderly, the communication with the library was direct; so that if a doubt or discussion was raised during lesson time (an event which the master never sought to discourage), information was readily to be had. The walls were decorated with specimens of the pupils' talents, less artistic than those in the library, but more rigidly useful. Maps, carefully copied ... all the work of the boys ... were sufficient stimuli to a healthy emulation.

wall display of children's work was quite rare hen this article was written, but the benefits of its e had obviously been recognized by some people. ompare this extract with the following two ncerning cheap boarding schools.

CHEAP BOARDING SCHOOLS

James Bryce reported on this kind of school for the Taunton Report in 1868. He considered that they were not:

... primarily a place of teaching, but a place of lodging and feeding. Boys are sent there to get them out of the way at home; boys, it may be, who have lost their mothers, or whose father is gone to America, or who are found unmanageable at home, or who have been lazy and neglected for several years, so that some desperate measure is needed to prepare them for an office in nine months time.

Why do you think some boys' fathers might have gone to America?

Bryce considered that for a boarding school to be cheap, either the food, the lodgings or the instruction must have been bad in order for the school still to make a profit. He went on to describe the rooms in one particular school:

Once in a bedroom 24 feet by 20, and as nearly as I could judge, 9 or 9½ feet high, there were 13 boys, that is about 350 cubic feet per boy. In another room in the same house the allowance was about 280 cubic feet per boy. A third room had a roof somewhat higher but the floor was covered with beds so thick that one could scarcely get in among them, and the boys must have had to dress and undress standing on their beds.

If the conditions in some of these schools were so appalling why do you think parents allowed their children to remain there? *Nicholas Nickleby* by Charles Dickens, first published in 1838/9, contains a bleak description of life in a nineteenth-century boarding school.

Church and Sunday Schools

The whole of Sunday was kept as a day of rest and prayer. All shops were closed and no form of sport or entertainment was allowed. At home, family prayers were read by the father and children had to read the Bible and sing hymns. Families would attend morning and evening service at church. Sometimes additional Sunday School classes were held in the afternoon for the children. The first Sunday Schools were set up for working children who were unable to attend schools during the week. Reading Bible stories and sometimes learning how to write were the main activities in these schools.

A short poem from The Infant's Magazine *1872, containing a religious message.*

LOVE ONE ANOTHER

Don't push the door, dear Katie,
But let your brother in;
To quarrel and to tease
Is wrong. It is a sin.

God tells us in His Word,
That we must *love each other,*

And it will grieve Him now,
If you're unkind to brother.

SUNDAY SCHOOL LESSONS

In his *Report on Manchester and the Textile Districts in 1849,* Angus Bethune Reach describes how the girls at St Paul's Sunday School, Manchester:

> . . . sat in classes, engaged, according to their progress, in reading Scripture or Scriptural extracts. One roomful was preparing to go to church and practising choral versions of the responses . . . [the girls] . . . ranged from

MEMORIES OF SUNDAY

Rose Smith was born in 1886 in Greenwich. She recalls visits to church and Sunday School when she was a child.

> We had to go to church three times on a Sunday, the morning, mid afternoon and the evening. We had to wear our best clothes and be on our best behaviour. The teacher sometimes took us up to her house for tea. They were all the gentry who ran the Sunday School in those days, not like today. You had to be gentry to teach at Sunday School. Once a year we went to Sevenoaks and Tunbridge Wells for our Sunday School outing. We went in brakes. They were large wagons drawn by horses. They had a roof but the sides were open. Every three months we had a Sunday School tea. We sometimes watched the magic lantern show in the evening when we joined the Band of Hope.

Whom does Rose mean by the "gentry"?

> little things of five and six . . . to well-grown young women. Many of them were the children of small shopkeepers and mechanics, the others were mill hands.

St Paul's was a Church of England Sunday School. Find out how your local Church of England Sunday School is organized today.

THE BAND OF HOPE

In the previous extract Rose Smith mentions that she was a member of the Band of Hope. The first

Children from London starting off on their annual Sunday School treat. Note the precarious position of some of the passengers in the wagon.

these Bands was formed in Leeds in 1847 to encourage the young to sign a pledge never to drink alcohol. Bands were usually affiliated to churches. Why do you think the young were recruited to this type of movement?

In Bush's *Budget and Directory of Bromley* (1894), there is this entry for the Plaistow Band of Hope:

> **Fortnightly meetings are held at 6.30 ... and a Tea for the children, followed by a social evening for the parents is given once a quarter. There is a Senior Division for boys from 13 to 17, and for girls from 14 to 18. The Band of Hope now numbers over 100 members.**

SUNDAY SCHOOL OUTINGS

Sunday School outings were usually held at Whitsuntide. The children were generally taken by train or wagon into the country or to the sea. In *The Growing Boy* (1967), Cecil Roberts describes one of the outings that took place at the turn of the century:

> **... we set out in four horse-drawn charabancs nearly a hundred strong guarded by a dozen voluntary teachers. ... It was my first trip in a charabanc and the height from the ground frightened me, although they had tied a rope across us. We set off at a smart pace, everybody on our charabanc singing Onward Christian Soldiers, though we were going to anything but the war.**

Does the custom of an annual outing still continue today?

Clothes and Appearance

Most Victorian children were dressed in a way that made them appear to be miniature versions of their parents. For most of the nineteenth century there were no special clothes designed for children. Girls wore long, full-skirted dresses and boys wore replicas of their fathers' suits. Many layers of clothing were worn regardless of the weather or of children's activities. It was considered improper for girls to show any bare leg, and so thin trousers called pantaloons were worn under dresses. Pinafores were often worn to disguise dirty, worn dresses or to save newer ones from excessive wear. Poor children wore whatever they could obtain, without any consideration of fashion. Many paupers lived permanently in thin rags and without any footwear.

THE RIGHT SHAPE

Girls from more affluent families often wore stays or a corset as they grew older. This was to make their waists look slim, but acquiring a so-called "fashionable" shape was often an ordeal:

> **Margaret says that the first time she was put into them – when she was about thirteen – she ran round and round the nursery screaming with rage. . . . I simply went away and took them off; endured sullenly the row which ensued, when my soft-shelled condition was discovered; was forcibly re-corsetted; and, as soon as possible went away and took them off again . . . to me they were real instruments of torture; they prevented me from breathing and dug deep holes into my softer parts on every side.** (Gwen Raverat, *Period Piece*, published in 1952)

Why would some young girls want to wear stays if they were so painful? Imagine playing tennis or cycling whilst wearing them.

THE WELL-DRESSED YOUNG LADY

Laura Troubridge stayed with friends in London in 1875 when she was 17. *Life Amongst the Troubridges* contains extracts from her journals and

A fashion illustration from Girl's Own Paper, *1888. The dresses are shorter versions of adult styles. Can you detect the young boy amongst the girls?*

memoirs. In her entry for 2 June 1875 she lists the clothes that had been packed for the visit to London:

> **My last summer's grey, turned and refurbished. My old peacock cashmere evening, transformed into a day gown with long sleeves and a front piece of the same. A white piqué (originally Confirmation), trimmed with frills and bouillonées of white lawn – and that's all day gowns. For the evening, a black tarlatan, high, long sleeves, white fichu and a train (my first), also rather a pretty muslin, with a nice little train, square and elbow sleeves . . . and my**

BREECHING

Up to the age of three or four, boys, like girls, wore dresses. Then they were "breeched" and allowed to wear trousers. In *Time and Again,* Helen Thomas remembers this about her younger brother, born in the 1880s:

> . . . on his third birthday he was promoted from frocks and petticoats to a sailor suit and . . . papa was cross when somebody seeing him in his male attire said, "Oh, I always thought he was a little girl."

CLOTHING CLUBS

Clothing clubs enabled poorer families to save a little money regularly in order to buy clothes. This evidence given to the Special Assistant Poor Law Commissioners on the Employment of Women and Children in Agriculture (1843) shows how useful these clubs were in country districts.

> I think that the children cannot be said to be badly clothed; they are warmly clad generally; the clothing clubs have greatly added to their comforts; at the same time these clubs have shown what a small regular saving will effect. . .

How can clothes be bought in a similar way today?

> dreadful yellow that I don't see myself wearing at all.

Cashmere, piqué and tarlatan are types of fabric. A bouillonée is a puffed fold, a fichu is a small lace shawl and a train is the long part of a skirt which trails on the ground at the back.

A boy wearing the sailor suit popularized by the Royal Family. The five-year-old Prince of Wales started the trend in 1846 when he wore a copy of Naval uniform on a visit to Ireland.

POOR CHILDREN IN LONDON

In *London Labour and the London Poor* (1861) Henry Mayhew describes the appearance of many poor children living in the capital. One boy:

> . . . had no shirt and no waistcoat; all his neck and a great part of his chest being bare. A ragged cloth jacket hung about him, and was tied, so as to keep it together, with bits of tape. What he had wrapped round for trousers did not cover one of his legs while one of his thighs was bare. He wore two old shoes: one tied to his foot with an old ribbon, the other a woman's old boot. He had an old cloth cap. His features were distorted somewhat through being swollen with the cold.

Thousands of children would be dressed similarly in rags in contrast to the few fortunate enough to have a wardrobe like that of Laura Troubridge.

Toys and Games

Poor and rich children alike were able to play games out-of-doors which involved little or no expense at all. Marbles, spinning tops, jacks, whips, hoops, skipping ropes and ball games were all very popular. A number of toys had been invented with the aim of instructing as well as amusing children, but only wealthier families could afford them. As improvements in industrial technology made mass-production possible, scientific, mechanical and optical toys appeared in large quantities. Nurseries in large houses usually contained a rocking horse. Dolls' houses and cardboard model theatres were other favourite toys. Many of these toys were made by hand so well by craftsmen that they have survived until today.

SPINNING TOPS

Spinning tops were popular toys. They were cheap, easy to carry around and could be spun on any flat surface without a lot of skill. Edward Thomas describes tops and other street games in his autobiography:

> In the hard asphalt playground we played rounders and egg-cap and games with tops, marbles and cherry-stones. Going home we spun our tops or two of us helped ourselves along by bowling hoops. . . . Tops, chiefly peg tops, we played endlessly. We tried to destroy our opponent's top by casting our own at it. . . . Or we strove against one another at hurling our tops out of the string a long distance, yet so that they should be spinning when they came to a standstill. The best spinners

RHYMING GAMES

Many games were peculiar to a particular area. No-one knew for how long they had been played or how they had originated. Girls often chanted rhymes to accompany their actions. In *Lark Rise to Candleford*, published in 1939, Flora Thompson describes a favourite game.

> A pretty, graceful game to watch was 'Thread the Tailor's Needle'. For this two girls joined both hands and elevated them to form an arch or bridge, and the other players, in single file and holding on to each other's skirts, passed under, singing:

> always threw their tops with the pegs pointing away from the ground instead of towards it, which I could never achieve or understand. (*The Childhood of Edward Thomas*)

Why would street games have been safer than they are today? Which street or playground games are popular in your area today?

A game of spinning tops in a London street c. 1900. ➤

Thread the Tailor's needle,
Thread the Tailor's needle,
The tailor's blind and he can't see,
So thread the tailor's needle.

As the end of the file passed under the arch the last two girls detached themselves, took up their stand by the original two and joined their hands and elevated them, thus widening the arch and this was repeated until the arch became a tunnel.

ny was a Victorian tailor likely to damage his ht? Which similar rhyming games have you yed? How did you learn them? What is the aning of the rhymes? Do you think the words ve been changed very much over the years?

A toy oarsman and boat with clockwork mechanism made in 1869. It is easy to see why toys with moving parts like this one became so popular.

PENNY BAZAARS

Time and Again, Helen Thomas describes the eat variety of toys that she was able to buy with r pocket money at a penny bazaar in the 1880s:

... you could buy little Japanese fans, tiny soft dolls with china head, hands and feet and a mop of black china curls. A bunch of six slate pencils each wrapped with pretty paper to hold, or a wooden lead pencil with a peep-hole at the top through which you could see a view of Southport. Fragile coloured glass bangles and packets of gay beads to thread. Useful things too – a design on a card pricked with holes and a skein of silk to embroider it with.

member that a Victorian penny was worth much ore than one penny is worth today. How much do u think some of these items would cost today?

CHARACTERS

One game that is still played today was that of "Characters" or "Twenty Questions", which proved to be very popular with young and old alike. This description is taken from Cassell's Family Magazine, 1880:

... one of the company thinks of some one particular person or thing, and the others ply him with questions, and endeavour to find out his secret from the answers. . . . Sometimes the company divide themselves into two parties, each of which sends out one of their number, and on his return questions him separately, and endeavours to find out his secret before the other side can do so.

Try and find out which of your favourite party games were played in the past by your parents and grandparents. If you have a card game called "Happy Families" look carefully at the cards, which are probably copies of original Victorian illustrations.

Hobbies

Without our modern-day diversions of radio and television, Victorian children usually found time for more creative pursuits. They were expected to amuse themselves in a quiet and worthwhile manner without distracting adults. Collecting was just as popular then as it is today. Filling scrapbooks was a relatively cheap and easy pastime and collecting birds' eggs, shells, pressed wild flowers and grasses was looked upon as having educational value. Girls were expected to be competent needlewomen, and samplers, showing the range of their embroidery stitches, were often framed and hung on the wall.

THE BICYCLING CRAZE

In *Period Piece*, published in 1952, Gwen Raverat describes her early bicycing experiences in Cambridge during the 1890s.

> **At first even 'safety' bicycles were too dangerous and improper for ladies to ride, and they had to have tricycles. . . . I found it very hard work, pounding away on my hard tyres; a glorious but not a pleasurable pastime. Then . . . my father said he had seen a new kind of tyre, filled up with air, and he thought it might be a success.**

Why do you think cycling became so popular so quickly?

COUNTRY PLAYTIME

In *Lark Rise to Candleford*, published in 1939, Flora Thompson tells how the village girls made "pin-a-sights" in the summer. These were flower petal

Collecting puzzles, riddles and sayings was a favour[ite] pastime. This page comes from a book of them collected by a teenage girl.

arrangements pressed between two small sheets [of] glass and covered by a brown paper flap.

> **Sometimes in the summer the 'pin-a-sights' were all the rage, and no girl would feel herself properly equipped unless she had one secreted about her. . . . Sometimes . . . they would . . . knock at a door, singing:**
>   **A pin to see a pin-a-sight,**
>   **All the ladies dressed in white.**
>   **A pin behind and a pin before,**

EVENINGS AT HOME

...ring the evening families usually stayed in one ...om to conserve both light and heat. George ...rt, described his evenings in *A Small Boy in the* ...*ties*:

> Perhaps our usual pastime was to sit round the light, prattling over our various little jobs – my sisters at their needlework or doll-dressing, myself with a pair of scissors 'cutting out' figures for scrap books. We sometimes played games, and if the games involved a little dressing-up, so much the better.

...hat medical condition would be a likely outcome ...children reading or amusing themselves in poor ...ht?

MAKING CHRISTMAS PRESENTS

...e making of "home-made" presents was more ...pular in Victorian times than it is today. The ...lowing suggestions were printed in the ...cember 1877 issue of *Little Folks Magazine*. They ...ideas for Christmas gifts for "mamma".

> And a pin to knock at the lady's door. They would then lift the flap and show the "pin-a-sight" for which they expected to be rewarded with a pin. . . . There was always a competition as to who should get the longest row of pins.

...e countryside provided many free games and ...ersions in the summer months. How would the ...dren living in the countryside have amused ...mselves in the winter?

A sampler by Elleanor Mahon from a book of school needlework exercises. It was worked in Ireland in 1854.

> The boys can give her ornamental brackets for her room, or frames for their own and sisters' photographs; the elder sister should make her a lovely white satin sachet for her pocket handkerchiefs, whilst the younger ones might accomplish a glove box of painted card, wadded, and bound with ribbon.

No actual instructions were given for the making of these items. Perhaps it was assumed that the children would be enterprising and talented enough to make them without any assistance.

Entertainment

Street entertainers provided a much sought after and free diversion for many children. Parades, fairs, carnivals and circuses were also relatively cheap forms of entertainment. Theatre or music hall visits were considered unsuitable for children but an annual visit the pantomime was essential for most midd and upper-class children. Magic lantern show were extremely popular. Drawn or painte and later, photographically produced slid were a source of wonder and amusement many families viewing in their homes or groups of children watching in church school halls.

A STREET SCENE IN FARNHAM

In his autobiography, *A Small Boy in the Sixties,* George Sturt describes the best place from which to view a dancing bear:

> To be sure, the shaggy docile creature padding along on its chain, behind the uncouth foreign-looking man who had tamed it, might be viewed more safely from upstairs. But the street was too narrow just there for a performance, and it was necessary to join the little crowd further along, to see the bear, immense on his hind legs, dance to the odd singing notes of the keeper with the long stout staff.

PENNY GAFFS

James Greenwood reckoned the "penny gaff" to one of the evils of Victorian London. The gaffs put plays that glamorized the lives of highwaymen thieves. Greenwood tried to highlight the l influence they had on children:

> Every low district has its theatre, or a least an humble substitute for one, called in vulgar parlance [speech] a 'gaff'. A gaff is a place in which . . . stage plays may not be represented. The actors of a drama may not correspond [communicate] in colloquoy [conversation], only in pantomime, bu the pieces brought out at the 'gaff' are seldom of an intricate character and the not over-fastidious auditory [audience] are well content with an exhibition of dumb show and gesture, that even the dullest comprehension may understand. . . . They are all children who support the gaff . . . (*The Seven Curses of London,* 1869)

The plays were very popular with the worl children. Can you think why? Why do you th Greenwood thought that plays and stories ab highwaymen and thieves would be a bad influe on children? Do you think he was right?

A performing bear and its trainer in the streets of St Mary Cray, Kent c. *1900. This would have been a very common sight at that time.*

HOW TO GIVE A CHILDREN'S PARTY

A different type of entertainment was that made at home. *Cassell's Family Magazine* of 1880 offered many suggestions for the organization of a successful children's party. This particular extract, though, describes what parents should not do:

> **What can be more ridiculous than to collect together a crowd of children, of all ages and dispositions, to exchange for five or six hours their well-ventilated nurseries for heated rooms and draughty passages; their simple food for indigestible pastry and sickly, unwholesome sweets; their ordinary warm clothing for low-necked sleeveless dresses, which leave exposed that most sensitive part of the human frame, the upper part of the arms and**

Enjoying a magic lantern show. Slides showing scriptural, foreign, humorous, war and natural history views were shown. What is being used for the screen in this photograph?

> **the chest; and then to allow them to sit up for two or three hours beyond their usual time for retiring, until the fashionable hour arrives for children's parties to break up...**

What sort of children did the writer have in mind? It appears from this advice that all the things children enjoy about parties were not to be allowed!

THE GOOSE FAIR

Every October the Goose Fair was held in the Market Place in Nottingham. In *The Growing Boy* (1967) Cecil Roberts remembers a particular novelty that he experienced there at the turn of the century.

> **It was called "The Animated Picture Show". You paid twopence and entered a dark tent. At the far end there was a white sheet. Suddenly the lights went out and from a hole in a box behind there came a beam of light that hit the screen. Someone began to play a lively tune on a piano. One could hear the whirring of the projector in the box. On the screen very black figures appeared and walked rapidly with jerky steps.... One felt one had seen a miracle for twopence. No one had spoken a word,**

> **the titles and dialogue flashed on and off the screen ... the queue outside the tent never ended. It was the event of the fair.**

Of what type of entertainment was this the forerunner?

Visiting fairs and local entertainment were often reported in local newspapers. You may find examples of some in your area.

Children's Literature

Many classic books were originally published in serial form during the last century. The work of Charles Dickens was often read aloud in weekly or fortnightly instalments to the whole family. Other authors who made a lasting impression were Lewis Carroll, Anna Sewell, Robert Louis Stevenson, Captain Marryat and Charles Kingsley. It was Kingsley who, in *The Water Babies*, brought the plight of young chimney sweep "climbing boys" to the attention of the public. Comics and periodicals were extremely popular during the second half of the century. Titles included *Little Folks, Girls' Own Paper* and *Boys of England*. Many of their stories contained references to Christian behaviour, happy family life and patriotic deeds. This moral element was looked upon favourably by parents.

PERIODICALS

Periodicals catered for all ages and interests. In *Shop Boy*, John Birch Thomas describes how, in the 1880s, he eagerly awaited the next instalment of a favourite story.

> **Granny gave me a penny a week to buy the Young Folks Budget. It came out every Thursday. There was a fine tale in it by Mr. Stevenson, called 'The Sea Cook'. I heard afterwards that it was made into a book and then they called it Treasure Island. I got it at the top of Morriston where they sold bottles of ink and tobacco and papers.**

Which periodicals do you buy today? Can you imagine any of the stories in them becoming future classics? How have newsagents changed since the description in this extract?

PENNY DREADFULS

In *The Seven Curses of London* (1869), James Greenwood laments the influence of "penny dreadfuls" or "gallows literature" on the impressionable young minds of London Children. Titles of this literature included *The Skeleton Band,*

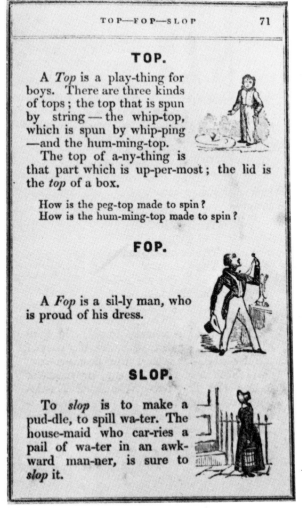

TOP—FOP—SLOP   71

TOP.

A *Top* is a play-thing for boys. There are three kinds of tops; the top that is spun by string — the whip-top, which is spun by whip-ping —and the hum-ming-top.
The top of a-ny-thing is that part which is up-per-most; the lid is the *top* of a box.

How is the peg-top made to spin?
How is the hum-ming-top made to spin?

FOP.

A *Fop* is a sil-ly man, who is proud of his dress.

SLOP.

To *slop* is to make a pud-dle, to spill wa-ter. The house-maid who car-ries a pail of wa-ter in an awk-ward man-ner, is sure to *slop* it.

◄ *A page from an infant's spelling book, 1844. The use of pictures in a text book had only recently been acknowledged as a valuable aid to learning.*

LITERATURE IN SCHOOL

Helen Thomas was a day pupil at a private elementary school in Southport in the 1880s. In *Time and Again* she describes the type of literature that the pupils were expected to read:

> The Pre-Raphaelites were well to the fore. We learnt the poems of Christina Rossetti and of Rossetti himself, some of Swinburne and of course Tennyson. At that time his Idylls of the King and his other poems were extremely popular; many girls were named Maude and many boys Lancelot [after the heroes and heroines].

Try to find out about the Pre-Raphaelite movement. Is the work of the poets mentioned in the extract still read in school today?

An illustration from Lucy's Wonderful Globe by Charlotte M. Yonge. She was a prolific author whose novels were full of girls ardently pursuing learning.

READING LESSONS

Reading was usually taught as a class lesson in school. Joseph Ashby described his experiences in a village school in the 1860s.

> Reading was worst; sums you did at least write on your slate, whereas you might wait the whole half-hour of a reading lesson while boys and girls who could not read stuck at every word. If you took your finger from the word that was being read you were punished by staying in when others went home. (*Joseph Ashby of Tysoe, 1859-1919*)

Why was this teaching method used? What are the disadvantages? How were you taught to read? What provision is there today for children with reading difficulties?

Tyburn Dick, Dick Turpin, The Boy Burglar and *Starlight Sall*. These were cheap comics that glamourized the lives of criminals. Greenwood complains that the literature is too immoral and crude for the young readers. Can you think of any modern equivalents that are supposed to have a bad influence on young people today?

Celebrations

Annual festivals, royal celebrations and victories in war were all celebrated by the Victorians. Festivals such as Christmas were celebrated in a similar way to the way they are today, with all the family gathered together enjoying themselves. Royal jubilees and the news of a victory in war usually meant a day's holiday, street parades and parties. Try and find out what wars were being fought during the Victorian period.

CHRISTMAS IN KENT IN 1874

In her diary, Eva Knatchbull Hugessen describes a Christmas party which took place on Saturday, 9 January 1874, much later than ours would be held today.

> In the afternoon we had our Christmas tree, we have been preparing it for days. . . . First we played "Old Soldier" and "Hunt the Slipper" in the schoolroom. Then Cousin Edith came to tell us that the tree was lighted and we all went into the drawing room. The tree looked very well, Arthur and Ned

DIAMOND JUBILEE

Queen Victoria celebrated her Diamond Jubilee on 22 June, 1897. All schools were given an extra day's holiday for the occasion. The proposed festivities for Chislehurst in Kent are typical of many that took place all over the country:

> . . . the children of the various schools shall have Jubilee medals presented to them. . . . They shall be worn on Tuesday June 22nd. . . . The children shall march from their different schools and assemble at the cockpit and shall

> cut the things off, and shouted the numbers [on the presents]. I had some very nice things, among others, a large box of preserved fruit, two boxes of chocolate creams, and a little sort of cardboard house which opened at the top and had some plaster doll's food in it.

It is thought that Prince Albert, Queen Victoria's husband, introduced the custom of the Christmas tree from his native Germany. The trees were lit by wax candles and decorated with small gifts. What parts of this extract tell you that it describes the celebrations of a wealthy family?

Farnborough Board School on the celebration of Queen Victoria's Diamond Jubilee. Miss Stocks, the Headmistress, wrote to the Queen congratulating her on the Jubilee and also thanking her for granting a day's holiday for all schools. She enclosed a copy of this photograph with her letter to the Queen.

> unitedly sing the National Anthem and the Old Hundredth, and shall then

SQUIB NIGHT

George Sturt describes how shop and house windows in Farnham, Surrey were boarded up in readiness for the 5 November celebrations.

> ... for the most part the squibs were homemade. For weeks beforehand boys were spending their leisure at that preparation – a sort of wicked cookery in which gunpowder, iron-filings, saltpetre and touch paper were the well-known ingredients boys discussed with one another. On the appointed night the products of this manufacture were slung round waist or neck in a bag or a tin cannister, for the 'guy' wearing it to get at easily in the dark.... A 'guy' probably wore a mask, and was covered fantastically in plenty of paper shavings and white or shiny paper, to show up suddenly if a squib was thrown down near one. (George Sturt, *A Small Boy in the Sixties*)

Is it legal to make your own fireworks today? The

Collecting a "Penny for the Guy" in Halstead, Essex, 1900. The photograph was taken by Edgar Tarry Adams. He was a wealthy businessman and photographer who lived and worked in Halstead.

boys' method of carrying their homemade squibs sounds very dangerous by today's standards. What precautions have been taken in recent years to prevent accidents. Do you know why we have fireworks on 5 November?

> march round the village and break off near their respective schools, where a tea shall be provided.... There is to be a fireworks display at 9.30, and a bonfire will be lit at 10 o'clock. Sports for the children will be arranged. (*Bromley Record*, 22 June, 1897)

Look in copies of your local newspapers for 1897 to find out how the Diamond Jubilee was celebrated in your area. Do you know any families who still have commemorative items which were presented to members of their family during the last century? On what occasions are extra school holidays granted today?

SCHOOL CELEBRATIONS

A problem concerning punctuality existed in the Board schools in Beckenham, Kent, until the following announcement was made:

> ... all those who attended punctually in the morning and afternoon with clean hands and faces, presented a tidy appearance, and were of good conduct should be present at the [Christmas] treat and receive gifts, and ... their parents should be allowed to attend.

There were hardly any unpunctual children after this announcement!

Going on Holiday

Easy travel by rail ensured that most people could enjoy holidays away from home, if only for a day, by the end of the nineteenth century. The Bank Holiday Act of 1871 gave six bank holidays a year. Before this the only holidays for workers were Saturday afternoons, Sundays and religious festivals. Middle- and upper-class families travelled either into the countryside or to the sea for their holidays, the seaside being the most popular destination. Sea-bathing and fresh coastal air were thought to promote good health. In the early years, male and female bathers used separate parts of the beach and bathing machines ensured even more privacy. As the century progressed, more families wanted to bathe together, and mixed bathing became acceptable. Cheaper rail fares made the one-day excursion very popular and many Londoners flocked to the coasts of Kent and Essex for a short break from their working lives.

GETTING AWAY FROM LONDON

For many children in the towns and cities a holiday in the country or by the sea was a rarity. These fortunate children from Rotherhithe had their holidays paid for by church-goers from Chislehurst in Kent.

> . . . sixty-two in all enjoyed the privilege (twenty-five to Stevenage, sixteen to Croydon, fifteen to Boxmoor and six to Sheerness). It is to help given by the Children's Holiday Fund that we are largely indebted for the opportunity of sending these children, for the fortnight's fresh air which is so necessary and so strengthening. In addition, however, many friends of the mission have responded to the appeal lately made by the Vicar, and thus on the last occasion fifty children more than otherwise could have gone, were

SCHOOL HOLIDAYS

Children at boarding school often lived a long way from home and so could only see their parents during the long summer break. The *Caterham School Magazine* of 1902 contains a pupil's reminiscences about his journey to the school which, until 1884, was situated in Lewisham, South London:

> A farmer friend lent his pony and my father drove me to Northampton, some fourteen miles. After spending the night in a friend's house, we took our places on the coach at eight a.m. for London, which we reached at about five-thirty. Again we spent the night with a friend, and next day took the Lewisham coach from Gracechurch St. to the Roebuck in Lewisham main street, and walked to the school. There was no Christmas home-going then for boys from a distance, and a few days'

sent . . . (Parish Magazine of Chislehurst and St Katherine's in Rotherhithe, 1889)

Does this particular type of charitable work still continue today?

Poor children from Deptford, London enjoying a day's holiday in the country. This event was organized by the Deptford Wesleyan Mission and paid for with a donation from an individual.

holiday at my London friends' was the only change from my ten months' life at Lewisham.

Roughly how long did the journey take? Find Northampton and Lewisham on a map. How long do you think it would take to travel from one to the other today?

TRAVELLING TO THE COUNTRY

Ellen Buxton lived in London but her family spent several months of the year with a grandmother who lived in Norfolk. In her diary Ellen describes their journey there:

"Sept 6. 1861 ... at nine the fly [carriage] came for us, and Papa, Mamma, Lisa, Johnney, Geof and I got into it and said good-bye to all the maids, and then drove off to Stratford station ... we had a very nice luncheon on the train at about twelve and when we had finished we tied up some pieces

A small audience watching the Punch and Judy show on Deal beach in 1900. This photograph was taken by Edgar Tarry Adams.

of bread etc. that we did not eat and tied them all up in paper parcels and then gave them away to some little boys. . . . We took Bully (the bullfinch) to Northrepps in his cage and he seemed to enjoy it, when we arrived at Norwich there was Grandmama's carriage all ready waiting for us.

BY THE SEA

Edward Thomas wrote about his family holidays in Eastbourne during the 1890s:

Our lodgings were small and uncomfortable and indoors we were always squabbling or annoyed our father. Out of doors all was well. We loafed about. . . . We threw pebbles about. We ate as much nougat as we could afford. . . . We rarely bathed, because we could not afford bathing machines every day and we could not swim and had not incitements to learn. (*The Childhood of Edward Thomas*)

Compare Edward's amusements with those available at the seaside today. What was the

purpose of a bathing machine? The expense of the machines did not prevent John Birch Thomas from swimming with his friends:

There were a lot of bathing machines up where most of the people went, but about a quarter of a mile on a deserted part towards the Mumbles there was a red mark down the sea-wall, and you were allowed to bathe there with nothing on. On hot days we brought bread and butter and a bottle of water and were naked savages all day ... some days we were too lazy to go as far as the red mark, but undressed where we oughtn't to. Then the bathing machine man would tell a policeman and we got chased. (John Birch Thomas, *Shop Boy*)

Diet

Diet improved towards the end of the century as doctors began to realize the relationship between health and an unbalanced diet. The main diet of the poor usually consisted of bread, potatoes, a small quantity of meat and occasionally some green vegetables. Cheap imported food and the introduction of commercial refrigeration meant that more dairy products and fruit were introduced into the diet of wealthy families. In some poor families it was customary to eat a sweet pudding before the actual dinner. This was to take the edge off everyone's appetite so that the meat of the main course would then go much further.

Children collecting soup and bread from a soup kitchen provided by the Deptford Wesleyan Mission in London.

SUBSIDISED MEALS

Cheap meals were available for some poor children. Others had free dinners paid for by local Children's Dinner Funds such as this one in South London:

> **The children's halfpenny dinners – and very good ones they are tho' the price is so low – have been resumed, and now take place on Tuesday, Thursday and Saturday.... On Tuesday and Saturday, the meal consists of a good bason of pea-soup with bread and pudding. On Thursday Irish stew (average ¼lb of meat per child) and bread is served.... Often more than 400 children are served on a day.** (Parish Magazine of Chislehurst and St Katherine's in Rotherhithe, 1889)

Despite the reference to low prices a large family may still have found it difficult to pay for the meals. Work out the weekly cost for a family with six children. Remember twelve pence equals one shilling.

DEATH CAUSED BY POOR DIET

By the end of the century the infant mortality rate was still high, even in areas considered to be quite healthy. The following is taken from the *Annual Report on Health in Beckenham, 1899*. Beckenham was a growing suburb of London.

> **Out of a total of 252 deaths registered, 96 were children under 5 years of age ... and no less than 78 of the 96 were amongst infants under the age of twelve months.... In a large proportion of these cases injudicious [unwise] infant feeding is in great measure responsible and a more correct appreciation of infantile dietetics**

EATING ON A LOW WEEKLY INCOME

In *Life As We Have Known It*, published in 1931; Welsh girl describes the diet of her family in the 1860s. Her father was a shoemaker who earned 12 shillings a week and her mother went out sewing, earning 1 shilling a day when she could find the work.

I also had to go two miles to a farmhouse for buttermilk, we could have as much as we could carry for 2d, ten to twelve quarts [2½ to 3 gallons] it was mostly. Our food then was potatoes and bacon, red herrings and bread and milk. There was no such thing as tea for the children in those days. Clear water we had to carry on our heads from some spring well.

FOOD FOR A WORKING BOY

A Report on the working conditions of children employed in agriculture (1867-8) gives us information about a working child's diet. For breakfast, Albert Merritt, aged ten, had:

. . . bread and cheese, and half a pint of cider.

would lead to a great saving of infant life. In these days there is no excuse for popular ignorance concerning this important subject.

Try to find out the figures for 1899 in your area. Ask your library if they have Medical Officers' Reports. If there is a marked difference between them and those quoted above try to identify the reason for this. The infant death rate was always at its highest in hot, dry summers. Can you think of a reason for this?

WEEKLY INCOME OF THE FAMILY.				WEEKLY EXPENDITURE OF THE FAMILY.			
	£	s.	d.		£	s.	d.
Nominal weekly wages of man, 16s.				Rent	0	3	0
				Candle	0	0	3½
Perquisites, 2s.				Bread	0	2	1
Actual weekly wages of man.	0	18	0	Butter..........	0	0	10
				Sugar	0	0	8
Nominal weekly wages of wife, 6s.				Tea	0	0	10
				Coffee	0	0	4
Perquisites in coal and wood, 1s. 4d.				Butcher's meat..	0	3	6
				Bacon	0	1	2
				Potatoes.......	0	0	10
Actual weekly wages of wife..	0	7	4	Raw fish........	0	0	4
				Herrings	0	0	4
Nominal weekly wages of boy..	0	3	0	Beer (at home)..	0	2	0
				,, (at work) ..	0	1	6
		1 8	4	Spirits.........	0	1	0
				Cheese	0	0	6
				Flour	0	0	3
				Suet............	0	0	3
				Fruit	0	0	3
				Rice............	0	0	0½
				Soap	0	0	6
				Starch..........	0	0	0½
				Soda and blue ..	0	0	1
				Dubbing	0	0	0½
				Clothes for the whole family, and repairing ditto	0	2	0
				Boots and shoes for ditto, ditto	0	1	6
				Milk	0	0	7
				Salt, pepper, and mustard	0	0	1
				Tobacco.........	0	0	9
				Wear and tear of bedding, crocks, &c.	0	0	3
				Schooling for girl	0	0	3
				Baking Sunday's dinner........	0	0	2
				Mangling	0	0	3
				Amusements and sundries......	0	1	0
					1	7	6

The weekly income and expenditure of a scavanger (street cleaner), his wife and their two children, taken from London Labour and the London Poor *by Henry Mayhew. Look at the items of food in the expenditure list. Compare them with the weekly shopping list for your family.*

At noon he had:

. . . a quarter of an hour for dinner, bread and cheese and cider.

Finally, his supper consisted of:

. . . potatoes and bacon, with nothing to drink.

What effect do you think the cider had on the boy's work? Compare this extract with your diet at the age of ten. What elements of a balanced diet are missing from this boy's meals?

Illness and Disease

Poor sanitation, an inadequate diet, and lack of medical attention, modern medical knowledge and drugs caused the rapid spread of disease and a high mortality rate among Victorian children. The living conditions of working-class children made them particularly vulnerable to infection, though children living in healthier areas were by no means exempt. Some rich children were delicate and, therefore, especially prone to tuberculosis.

EPIDEMICS

In Beckenham, Kent, a measles epidemic was reported by the Medical Officer for Health in 1898:

> **... upwards of one hundred children were infected during the epidemic ... eight deaths occurred from measles, a low rate of mortality considering the large number of cases. During former epidemics, the rate of mortality was very much higher and the cause for the high mortality was, I believe due to the very complacent [unconcerned] view taken by parents regarding measles.**

Would eight deaths be so readily accepted as a low rate today? In order to check the progress of disease many schools were closed and disinfected. You may find evidence of this in school log books.

SCHOOL INSPECTORS' REPORTS

The physical condition of some poor children was realized more fully after 1870 when school managers and inspectors reported on the health of children in Board schools. George Sturt wrote about the condition of the country children at the turn of the century:

> **Such defects as the doctor finds are**

INFANT MORTALITY

A high birth rate was accompanied by a high rate of mortality. Angus Bethune Reach, an investigative journalist for the *Morning Chronicle*, reported in 1849 that:

> **Out of every hundred deaths in Manchester more than forty-eight take place under five years of age, and more than fifty-one under ten years of age. In some of the neighbouring towns ... the proportion is still more appalling ... out of the whole number of deaths, fifty-seven per cent were those of children under five years of age.**

He attributed this undue proportion of infant deaths to the neglect of mothers who were compelled to leave their young children at home while they worked in the mills.

Different surroundings and standards of living were clearly reflected in child mortality rates. Try to find out if the health of your local area compared favourably with those mentioned here.

> **generally of no deep-seated kind: bad teeth, faulty vision (often due probably, to improper use of the eyes in school), scalp troubles, running ears, adenoids, and so on, are the commonest. Insufficient nutrition is occasionally reported. In fact the medical evidence tells, in a varied form, much the same tale that school managers have been able to read for themselves in the children's dilapidated boots and clothes and their grimy hands and uncared-for hair, for it all indicates poverty at home, want of convenience for decent living, and ignorance as well as carelessness in the parents.** (George Sturt, *Change in the Village*)

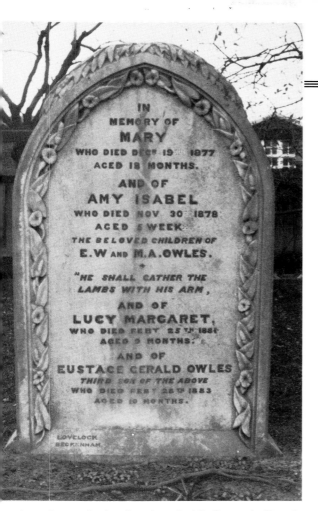

A tombstone in the churchyard of St George's Church in Beckenham, Kent which records the loss of four babies from the same family in less than six years. Look in your local churchyard for similar memorials to Victorian children.

DRUGGED CHILDREN

Angus Bethune Reach also found evidence to suggest that while the mothers were out working in the mills many young children were drugged with a sweetened preparation of laudanum which kept them quiet and made them easier to look after.

> An intelligent male operative [worker] in the Messrs. Morris's mill in Salford stated that he and his wife put out their first child to be nursed. The nurse gave the baby 'sleeping stuff' and it died in nine weeks.

A female worker in the mill at Chorlton described to the journalist the effects of the drugging:

> The child seemed to be always asleep and lay with its eyes half open. Its head got terribly big and its fingernails blue . . . it died very soon after.
> (*Manchester and the Textile Districts in 1849*)

Some mothers were also found to have drugged their own children. If the children were fortunate enough to survive this early drugging, what long-term effects might it have had on them?

HEALTHY HOMES

In *Every Day Cookery and Housekeeping Book* (1865) Mrs Beeton offers this advice to parents on the subject of health:

> Where it is possible, large airy rooms at the top of the house should be given up to the babies. A day and night nursery are required, and the night nursery should be the larger of the two. . . . Every room occupied by children should have a fireplace and chimney to allow of ventilation during the night. A large window is also requisite. In winter it is well to carpet the bedroom, but this should be removed at the spring cleaning. Once a week at least the bedroom fire should be lighted during the winter.

How do these arrangements compare with the conditions described in the previous extracts?

Map

Edinburgh

Washington

0   100
km

Lancaster

Leeds   York

Southport
Llandudno

Manchester

Nottingham

Sudbury

Norwich

Warwick

Northampton

Cambridge

Tring

Bath

LONDON   Bethnal Green
Lewisham   Greenwich
Beckenham   Bromley
Farnham   Caterham   Farnborough
Boughton
Manchelsea

Worthing

Eastbourne

KEY

| York | Places to visit. |

| Tring | Places mentioned in the text. |

Difficult Words

almshouse	privately supported home offering accommodation to the aged or needy.
bathing machine	small wooden hut on wheels which took bathers to the sea.
bazaar	market.
bodice	close-fitting upper part of a dress.
brake	large, horse-drawn wagon.
charabanc	large, motorized or horse-drawn wagon with seats.
corporal punishment	punishment of physical nature, such as flogging or beating.
corset	closely fitting inner bodice stiffened with whalebone and fastened by laces.
curriculum	all the subjects taught in school.
distemper	special paint used for murals and posters.
domestic service	working as a household servant.
enclosure	the enclosing of common land to make it private property.
gentry	people who come next below the nobility in position and birth.
gleaning	the gathering of corn ears left by the reapers.
governess	woman who teaches children in a private household.
hawker	someone who carries goods around for sale.
investigative journalist	someone who exposes issues and problems in newspapers.
legislation	Acts of Parliament which give us laws.
linsey-woolsey bag	bag made from a mixture of cotton and coarse wool.
magic lantern	forerunner of today's slide projector.
monitors	older children who helped with the teaching in schools.
nanny	child's nurse.
nursery	room where young children live and sleep.
oakum shed	where prisoners unpicked rope into loose fibres.
philanthropist	someone who loves and helps others.
recitations	repetition aloud of a poem or a piece of prose learnt from memory.
School Board	bodies of people appointed by the 1870 Education Act, responsible for building new schools in a particular area where there were none already, and for restoring the standard of existing schools.
slate	individual small blackboard used by children to write on.
spinning top	wooden or metal pear-shaped toy. It spins on a sharp point at the bottom when set into motion by hand or by string.
treadmill	form of punishment where prisoners moved a revolving cylinder by a stepping motion.

CONVERSION TABLE		
NEW MONEY		*OLD MONEY*
1p	=	*2.4d. (2.4 old pence)*
5p	=	*1s. (1 shilling)*
50p	=	*10s. (10 shillings)*
£1	=	*£1*
		12d = 1 shilling
		20 shillings = £1
£1.05	=	*21 shillings (a guinea)*

Date List

The following dates concern the education and the employment of children. Many Acts were passed concerning these two issues. Remember that it often took time for new laws to be enforced and that conditions for children were not improved overnight. In many of the Employment Acts instructions were complicated and so employers ignored them. Many parents and children also infringed the rules.

1840 One of many Chimney Sweep Acts forbidding the employment of children.
1842 Mines Act prevents children under ten from working underground.
1843 Factory Act introduces "half-time" system of education.
1844 Ragged School Union founded. Factory Act reduces children's hours in textile factories to six and a half a day. They are still able to start at the age of eight though.
1847 Ten Hours' Act. No women or young person aged between 13 and 18 to work in a factory more than ten hours a day.
1850 North London Collegiate School for girls founded by Frances Buss.
1862 Revised Code of Education sets up the system of "payment by results".
1868 Gangs Act forbids the employment of children under eight in gangs on the land.
1870 Forster's Education Act introduces Board schools.
1873 Agricultural Act preventing the employment of children under eight in any form of agriculture, except by their parents.
1875 Act allowing police to grant chimney sweeps a licence only if they are satisfied that they are not employing climbing boys.
1876 Minimum school leaving age fixed at ten.
1878 Consolidation Act. No child under eight to work in any trade. Children between eight and 13 can only work half-time.
1880 Schooling compulsory up to the age of ten.
1891 Elementary education becomes free.
1897 "Payments by results" abolished.
1902 Education Act replaces School Boards with Local Education Authorities.

Places to Visit

Many museums have collections of Victorian toys, games, books and costumes. Others may have reconstructions of period rooms or schoolrooms which also give an insight into the everyday life of Victorian children. Most exhibits will have belonged to wealthy children. The clothes and the toys of the poor have not lasted so well. Your local museum may have a collection of childhood artefacts from the surrounding areas. The following is a selection from some of the larger museums.

1. London
The Bethnal Green Museum of Childhood has an excellent collection of toys, games, children's costumes, dolls and dolls' houses.
The London Toy and Model Museum contains mechanical toys and models of means of transport.
The Museum of London has Victorian classroom furniture and exhibits on nineteenth-century education, such as good conduct and attendance medals. It also has a section on the poor who lived in the city.
2. York
The Castle Museum has reconstructions of Victorian rooms and displays of costumes and toys.
3. Bath
The Museum of Costume has displays showing how fashions changed during the nineteenth century.
4. Edinburgh
Museum of Childhood.
5. Llandudno
Doll Museum.
6. Sudbury Hall, Derbyshire
The Museum of Childhood contains a reconstruction of a classroom and a display about the Victorian child at work.
7. Warwick
Doll Museum. St John's house has a reconstruction of a Victorian classroom.
8. Nottingham
The Brewhouse Yard Museum contains furnished rooms of the Victorian period. The Museum of Costume and Textiles has examples of Victorian costume displayed in nineteenth-century period rooms.
9. Lancaster
The Museum of Childhood contains a Victorian schoolroom and exhibits of dolls, toys and games.

Biographical Notes

ASHBY, Joseph. The biography of his village life in Tysoe was written by his daughter.

GREENWOOD, James. An investigative journalist who wrote books describing the life of the poor in London.

HUGHES, M.V. The first three volumes of her autobiography describe growing up in Victorian London. They are very readable.

MAYHEW, Henry. Another investigative journalist who reported on the problems of the poor in London.

RAVERAT, Gwen. Her autobiography contains many amusing accounts of her childhood in Cambridge. She was part of a wealthy family. Her paternal grandparents were Charles Darwin and Emma Wedgewood.

REACH, Angus Bethune. Another journalist who exposed the conditions of the working poor in Victorian England.

STURT, George. Writer of an autobiography describing life in Farnham, Surrey in the 1860s. Sometimes wrote with the pen-name G. Bourne.

THOMPSON, Flora. Her account of country life in an Oxfordshire village at the end of the nineteenth century is very readable.

Book List

Modern Books

Carol Adams, *Ordinary Lives A Hundred Years Ago,* Virago, 1984

E. Allen, *Victorian Children,* A & C Black, 1973

Amanda Clarke, *Finding Out About Victorian Schools,* B.T. Batsford, 1977

Sheila Ferguson, *Growing Up in Victorian Britain,* B.T. Batsford, 1977

C. Ford and B. Harrison, *A Hundred Years Ago: Britain in the 1880s in Words and Photographs,* Penguin, 1983

J. Hughes, *A Victorian Sunday,* Wayland, 1972

D. Kennedy, *Past into Present: Children,* B.T. Batsford, 1971

Elizabeth Longmate, *Then and There: Children at Work 1830-1885,* Longman, 1981

S. Purkiss, *Into the Past: At School in 1900,* Longman, 1981

Michael Rawcliffe, *Finding Out About Victorian Country Life,* B.T. Batsford, 1984 and *Finding Out About Victorian Towns,* B.T. Batsford, 1982

P.P. Speed, *Then and There: Learning and Teaching in Victorian Times,* Longman, 1983

Gordon Winter, *A Country Camera 1844-1914,* Penguin, 1973

Sources of Extracts

M.K. Ashby, *Joseph Ashby of Tysoe 1859-1919,* Cambridge University Press, 1961

G. Avery, *The Echoing Green: Memories of Regency and Victorian Youth,* Collins, 1974 (this uses diaries of young people written at the time or their memories)

G. Avery (ed.) *Red Letter Days,* Hamish Hamilton, 1971 (memories of important days, mainly from the lives of nineteenth-century children)

John Burnett, *Destiny Obscure,* Penguin 1974 and *Useful Toil,* Penguin, 1982

Co-operative Working Women (ed. M. Llewelyn Davies), *Life As We Have Known It,* Chatto & Windus, 1931

James Greenwood, *Seven Curses of London,* first published 1869 (one of his "curses" was the plight of poor children living in the city)

J. Hope-Nicholson, *Life Among the Troubridges,* John Murray

M.V. Hughes, *A London Child of the 1870s, A London Girl of the 1880s,* Oxford University Press, *1934 A London Home in the 1890s,* Oxford University Press, 1946

Henry Mayhew, *London Labour and the London Poor,* first published by Griffin, Bohn and Company, 1861; reprinted by Dover Publications Inc, 1968

Gwen Raverat, *Period Piece,* Faber and Faber, 1952

Angus Bethune Reach, *Manchester and the Textile Districts in 1849,* Helmshore Local History Society, 1972

Cecil Roberts, *The Growing Boy,* Hodder and Stoughton, 1967

George Smith, *The Cry of the Children from the Brick-Yards of England,* 1879

George Sturt, *A Small Boy in the Sixties,* Caliban Books, 1982 and *Change in the Village,* 1912

Edward Thomas, *The Childhood of Edward Thomas,* Faber and Faber, 1938

Helen Thomas, *Time and Again,* Carcanet New Press, 1978

John Birch Thomas, *Shop Boy,* Routledge and Kegan Paul, 1983

Flora Thompson, *Lark Rise to Candleford,* Oxford University Press, 1939

Index

Adams, Edgar Tarry 37, 39
almshouses 8
Ashby, Joseph 17, 20, 35

Band of Hope 24, 25
Barnardo, Dr 4, 10
Beckenham 19, 37, 40, 42, 43
Beeton, Mrs 7, 43
Bethnal Green 5, 7
bicycling 30
birthdays 8, 9
boarding schools 22, 23, 38
Boughton Monchelsea 18
breeching 27
Bromley 7, 11, 13, 22, 25
Burke, Thomas 12
Buxton, Ellen 8, 39

carte de visite 8
Caterham 22, 38
celebrations 36, 37
Children's Employment
    Commission 12
Chislehurst 36, 38
Christmas 31, 36
church 24, 25
clothes 8, 26, 27
country 16, 17, 30

Diamond Jubilee 36
diaries 5, 8, 21, 26, 36, 39
Dickens, Charles 23, 34
diet 19, 40, 41
discipline 3, 18
dolls' houses 9
domestic service 12
drugs 43

education 3, 18, 19
entertainment 32, 33

family life 3, 6, 7
farming 16
Farnborough 11, 16, 20
fogs 15, 36
Forster Education Act 3, 18

foster parents 7

games 28, 29
gleaning 16
governesses 21
Greenaway, Kate 9
Greenwich 24
Greenwood, James 10, 14, 32, 34

half-timers 13
hobbies 30, 31
holidays 38, 39
hop-pickers 16
Hugessen, Eva Knatchbull 8, 21, 36
Hughes, Molly 15, 20

illness 42, 43
infant mortality 4, 42
inspectors 18, 19, 42

Kingsley, Charles 34

lessons 20, 21
Lewisham 22, 38
literature 34, 35
Little Lord Fauntleroy 8
Liverpool 12
log books 5, 11, 17, 18, 20
London 7, 10, 14, 15, 27, 32, 34, 38

magic lanterns 19, 32, 33
Manchester 12, 24, 42
Mayhew, Henry 7, 10, 14, 15, 19, 27, 41
measles 42
mudlarks 15

nannies 6, 9
Northampton 38
Nottingham 33
nurseries 7, 8, 9

object lessons 20

parties 33, 36
Payment by Results 18, 20
penny bazaars 29

penny gaffs 32
periodicals 34
philanthropists 4
pickpockets 10
poor 4, 10, 11, 14, 17, 27
presents 8, 9, 31, 36
punishments 3

ragged schools 19
Ravarat, Gwen 9, 26, 30
Reach, Angus Bethune 12, 24, 42, 43
recitations 20
Revised Code of Education 18
rich children 8, 9, 26
Roberts, Cecil 25, 33
rookeries 14

samplers 31
school treats 17
schools 18, 19, 20, 21, 22, 23
Shaftesbury, Lord 4
shoeblacks 12
slums 10, 19
Smith, George 13
spinning tops 28
Sturt, George 31, 32, 37, 42
Sunday school 24, 25

Taunton Report 23
Ten Hours Act 12
Thomas, Edward 15, 22, 28, 39
Thomas, Helen 27, 29, 35
Thomas, John Birch 34, 39
Thompson, Flora 12, 28, 30
Tottenham 23
toys 28, 29
transportation 10
Tring 11
Troubridge, Laura 26

Washington 19
workhouse 7, 10, 11, 13
working children 12, 13
Worthing 6

Yonge, Charlotte M. 35

Acknowledgments continued from p. 2.

page 15 from *A London Child of the 1870s* and on page 20 from *A London Girl of the 1880s* both by M.V. Hughes; Penguin for the extracts on pages 11 and 19 from *Useful Toil* by J. Burnett; D. Pullen for the photographs on pages 4 and 27; Michael Rawcliffe for photographs on pages 10, 14, 16, 21, 25, 28, 33, 34, 38 and 40; P. Richards for the photograph on page 8; Routledge Kegan Paul for

extracts on pages 34 and 39 from *Shop Boy* by John Birch Thomas; The Society of Authors for extracts on pages 25 and 33 from *The Growing Boy* by Cecil Roberts; P. Taylor for the photographs on pages 6, 24, 26 and 35; Mrs Myfanwy Thomas for extracts on pages 15, 22, 28 and 39 from *The Childhood of Edward Thomas* by Edward Thomas and on pages 27, 29 and 35 from *Time and Again* by Helen Thomas. The map on page 44 was drawn by R.P. Brien.